SUMMARY
& REVIEW
OF
ISABEL WILKERSON'S
CASTE

The Origins of Our Discontents

High Speed Reads

TABLE OF CONTENTS

THIRTY SECOND SUMMARY

We love to think that we here in America are the freest, happiest people on the planet, but that simply isn't the case, and for more than one reason. For one thing, we're not statistically the happiest country in the world by a long shot. We're not even the freest country. The reason for this lies in how we treat everyone in this country who isn't white. Slavery may have ended, but the national attitude toward African Americans has definitely not. In a country where black people have to deal with oppression, suppression, off-balance violence and police brutality and economic instability, we are definitely not past what can be defined as the caste system of America, the very structure upon which it was founded and which it now subtly relies on today.

In Caste: The Origins of Our Discontents, by Isabel Wilkerson, we're going to go on a fantastic and heartbreaking journey of the reality of African Americans of today and the plights of their enslaved ancestors of yesteryear. You'll learn where the prominent racial issues of today ultimately stemmed from and how those issues are threatening to not only tear this country apart, but also the very people whom they affect so strongly on both sides of the debate. You'll also learn the consequences of major racial upheavals in government and just what effect they had long after they'd ended. It's a book written to open the eyes of the American citizens to the reality of the caste system that still governs us and why it must be eliminated from our culture.

PROLOGUE: THE MAN
IN THE CROWD

In a shipyard, graced by the light of the sun, a hundred or so workers can be seen in an old black and white photo, one of whom stands out from the others. He stands out amidst the crowd of people performing the infamous Nazi salute, hands stretched to the sky. His own arms are folded. He stood against the tide. People believe his name was August Landmesser. He had clearly had enough of the hate-filled air around him. He had joined the Nazi party and clearly now felt disillusioned by it. He saw the Jews as human when so many others refused to. He had been in love with a Jewish woman, but the Nuremberg Laws made this relationship illegal. He was forbidden to marry her. He was brave to stand against the tide in such a manner.

We all like to believe that we could stand against such unfairness and toxicity ourselves, but being brave is much harder than it sounds. Discomfort, derision, internal and external fears and social judgement must all be overcome in order to stand against such toxic solidarity. So, with such devastating risks abound, just what would it take to follow in August's footsteps in today's times?

PART ONE

TOXINS IN THE PERMAFROST AND HEAT RISING ALL AROUND

CHAPTER 1: THE AFTERLIFE
OF PATHOGENS

2016 was a tough year. You'd be hard pressed to find anyone who disagrees with this statement. But for the herdsmen of the Russian peninsula of Yamal, an unprecedentedly hot summer brought with it a strange illness that bore down on their children like a plague, a strange disease they'd never seen before. The Nenet people watched their gravely sick children get airlifted to a hospital in Salekhard, where several passed away. It was discovered that the rampant heatwave had dug down deep into the permafrost where a vein of anthrax from 1941 had been imprisoned within the carcasses of victimized reindeer. The pathogen spores had never died, simply lying in wait until they reawoke during a time of opportunity.

Extreme circumstances restored it to the surface.

This extreme circumstance came into similar light across the world where an election of devastating division and derision rose like the heat. People found their country unrecognizable, now. With two such divisive candidates, a politically inclined woman and a socially awkward billionaire, America's tensions were rising. The male candidate was pursuing all sorts of unethical jabs at his opponent, his followers growing more manic. Everyday interactions became rife with a black and white mentality of choosing a side with no middle ground to be seen. All of this tension had been churning below the surface as a result of the previous election producing the first president of color. When 2016's election brought forth a candidate who was open about criticizing this previous leader, it allowed for a lot of underground opinions to begin rising to the surface. And while the popular vote showed a win for the female candidate, the Electoral College decided that the male candidate would take the win.

Now, the United States was grounded in a course to last for possible years, in which isolationism and tribalism would become focal points of society and wealth and power were worshipped like golden idols, where the health of all others, even Earth itself, was second to the gathering of material items. For many, with the succession of the billionaire to the seat of power, a time where 'everybody knew their place' was rapidly coming. Hate and violence became rife. Immigrants saw injury and death, a white navy veteran was convicted of domestic terrorism for killing a black elderly man with a sword in New York, three men were attacked for defending a Muslim girl on a train, and so on. 2017 saw more mass shootings than at any other point in time. Treaties were pulled by the president, the US withdrew from the Paris Agreement and things only seemed to be getting worse.

By the third year, he found himself impeached, but not removed. Finally, in 2020, the Covid-19 pandemic struck the world, wherein the president handwaved it away as "The Chinese virus" and refused to take it seriously. Medical equipment was scarce and nothing was being done federally. The state governments left to their own devices. As time went by, federal agents were observed removing supplies from state government stations. The country had run out of monocles to pop. Shock was just part of everyday life now, leaving many to question what had happened to the country. What was so vital to his voters that many would place their trust and safety in the hands of a game show host?

It was an earthquake of a different sort, a mad dash for power and wealth. A desire for something of the past brought present. They are quakes caused by our own hidden desires, at the very center of our unease. Like the anthrax that awakened with drastic circumstances in Russia, so too did our societal unrest that we'd buried decades ago. It hadn't gone anywhere. It was always there. It just took a loud and unusually powerful force to awaken it and force it back to the surface. We cannot escape our history forever. It's only a matter of time until it comes back to claim us.

CHAPTER 2: AN OLD HOUSE AND
AN INFRARED LIGHT

I saw the old house as a mystery to be solved, a decrepit piece of the past that can never be truly fixed. I view the country the same way. America has a lot of buried history in its original construction that we're still struggling to repair today. Whatever problems you face *must* be faced whether you like it or not. If we live in this modern world, we get to tackle the problems that world comes with. It's our responsibility to try to make any repairs we can, as well as accept whatever else goes wrong while it's in our hands. Problems won't fix themselves.

For America, one of those problems is its underlying infestation of the old caste system, the system of rank that humans encoded into society based on dominant traits and features imposed by people possessing those same features. Systems like the Nazi party, India as a whole, and of course, the US, where those deemed inferior are stigmatized and downtrodden upon for being born in the 'wrong' caste. These rules are embedded into the beings of those they're imposed upon to justify any number of cruel acts against the lower ranking people. In America, people of color are considered lower on the old caste system. It's invisible. We don't even know we're doing it half the time. That's how prevalent it still is today.

We are born into this infestation, this centuries' old problem, and its invisible demands on our society. And it becomes our responsibility to address this and other problems, face it, and work to correct it.

CHAPTER 3: AN AMERICAN UNTOUCHABLE

Martin Luther King Jr. had always dreamed of visiting India with his wife Coretta and they stayed there for a month upon invitation to visit by Prime Minister Jawaharlal Nehru. King had found his inspiration to fight the ingrained American caste system by watching a similar fight happening in India against British rule. His reputation of his fight for freedom preceded him and he was swarmed by touched fans. He visited a high school filled with relations of former Untouchables. He was announced by the Principal as an Untouchable himself, shocked to hear the title attached to his own name. However, as he thought about it some more, he realized that it made sense that they would see an American Negro as a low caste like themselves. He thought of his people back home languishing in poverty and ghettos and came to the understanding that he and all Black Americans back home were Untouchables in their own right. He was opened to America's own ingrained caste system.

The caste system rose as the country of America neared its birth, as men came to view what they wanted as their 'right' and that they had the right to take such things. They viewed the people living in their coveted land as either property to be claimed or nuisances to be disposed of. Their Bible was interpreted in the ways they saw fit and they used it to justify their 'dominance'. Twelve generations of captured Africans shipped off from their homelands to build the new world introduced the European caste system we now understand today. The ideation that how a person looked on the outside would unwittingly become the foundation of the free world, an invisible network of expectations that the people were expected to follow. To understand the upheavals of today, it's crucial to look back at this dark foundation first. The race problem in America can be traced all the way back to this manufactured belief in the superiority and inferiority in races.

The American caste system is a hierarchy artificially constructed to place people in society based on their appearances. To help illustrate the issues of the American system, it's possible to look at India's and see the similarities therein, as well as the concentration of caste and superiority complexes that made up the Nazi party. In 1619, the American caste system began with the first black slaves brought to Virginia. Europeans were sorted into the 'white' category, the diametric opposite of the 'black' category. Most of this early determination of the caste system took place in the South, which is why that section of the country will be most heavily referenced when speaking about the caste system. Where better to start with the issue than at the source?

PART TWO

THE ARBITRARY CONSTRUCTION OF HUMAN DIVISION

CHAPTER 4: A LONG-RUNNING PLAY AND THE EMERGENCE OF CASTE IN AMERICA

We are all actors, wearing costumes that can never be removed, acting on a stage we can never leave. The roles are passed down generationally and the actors are encouraged to adopt the new persona as their very person. This is the caste system of America. It's a performance. Many adjust flawlessly to it. Many others don't, and therefore struggle to keep up appearances of the character they've been assigned. Not everyone is born to be an actor, after all. No one can fully agree exactly how the play began, whether the black actors involved were forced into immediate and lifelong servitude to the show, or if it had been planned as a temporary performance. But they've been here for over two hundred years, so regardless, they're committed to the role. We've all been cast into roles from the moment we're born and only death can remove us from the stage. So what do we do in the meantime?

The first Africans arrived in 1619 at Point Comfort on the east coast, which would later become Virginia. They had been purchased from slave ships heading to the Spanish Colonies. Almost immediately, they were indoctrinated into the early caste system, and over decades and centuries, this same caste system would not only help to become the root of American politics and economics, but also its most crippling and destabilizing feature. Early Africans weren't even included in the censuses of the time. Back then, religion ruled over race, and this is what tended to extinguish indigenous people that the white Europeans came across. However, Africans challenged the caste here and there by converting to Christianity, counterbalancing the desire for cheap labor by the ruling classes. The Africans were a strong, hardy and somewhat docile people which stood out from the crowd. As the Indigenous people were pushed out for their weaker natures, this left the Africans at the mercy of the bottom rung of the caste system.

Many Americans don't like to talk about slavery because they believe it was little more than a chapter of history. But the only way to truly rebuild and heal the damage being done to the country, and to reach a peace with those still being affected, is to examine and embrace the full history. Slavery wasn't just a single chapter, it was essentially the basis for the founding of the country and its economy. It was a part of life and it made life out here possible. We've clearly found other ways of succeeding without direct slavery these days, but there's no denying the sheer force it had on the development of early America. Slaves were treated terribly, they faced injury, death and harassment. This terrible treatment continued for centuries, even after slavery had ended. Blacks still came under restrictions, especially in the south and this didn't come into question until well into the 1960's. It just goes to show that even with slavery at an end, the caste system is still very much in evidence.

CHAPTER 5: THE CONTAINER WE HAVE BUILT FOR YOU

Even as early as 1965, the caste system was rife. A young woman named Miss recounted the meaning behind her unusual name and her father's fight to keep his house and home looking well in the deep south. She had been named such that people would be forced to refer to her as both her name and her title, which had been denied all her ancestors of either gender. Her father worked his whole life subtly battling threats to his passions in the form of destruction of his home, such as grounding his mailbox in concrete so that arms were wrenched every time someone tried to whack it with a baseball bat. She recounted how she'd agitated her high school principal who had to get her records to prove that her name was indeed Miss, the one word he'd been taught his whole life to never address a black woman as. Her father had lived for this moment, and told her to live up to her name to its fullest extent. Another time, she had the chance to spend time with a northern family who found her name and its story hilarious and were thrilled at the effect it had had. The matriarch of the family wished that Miss would have stayed and remarked softly how a time once existed when she could have made her stay.

Miss mentioned a container, one created for her and all black Americans by society, and how, for the most part, society was okay with her, so long as she stayed within that container. Honestly, each of us exists in a container of sorts. I, myself, was once accused of being an imposter...for *myself* during an interview for *The New York Times*, where I used to work. I was aggressively shoved away, with the man's expectations of a "container" from the prestigious paper coming in a package that I suppose wasn't going to look how I did. The root of the problem goes much deeper than one crabby exception to the now generally accepted rule.

CHAPTER 6: THE MEASURE
OF HUMANITY

Perhaps in an alternate world, people were grouped in castes not for color, but for height variations. Preconceived notions about the benefits of one height or another, the strengths and weaknesses and the idea that tall people are better at physical labor and sports, but aren't as smart and the like. Sound ridiculous? It shouldn't. That's basically what we did with skin color and different races. The concept of race is a fairly new development and likely harkens back to *raza*, the Spanish word used to refer to castes regarding horse breeds. It's now used as an unbendable measure for worth amongst people in many countries, particularly in North America. It determines one's worth in a social standing and cannot be overcome normally.

Similarly, the word caucasian as used to describe white people is fairly recent, coming from a skull in the possession of Johann Friedrich Blumenbach, which came from the Caucasus mountains in Russia. He found the skull beautiful and pristine, and so he called its group of Europeans under the name Caucasians after the region from whence it came. And this is where the random name of Caucasian came from for white people.

In the advent of DNA testing kits, we now know that race as we have come to know it is entirely fiction. A person can look white, but be able to trace their origins to any number of different places on the globe, some thousands of miles apart. In the end, we're basically all mutts. Science has proven that we all ultimately came out of Africa and migrated across the world, adapting to the myriad of new environments we encountered, our skins changing to match those environments over millennia. The concept of race is not only fictional, it's purely a societal concept. We accept it only because we've been told to.

Now, as things get more wild and unpredictable, the word racism has become a "dirty" word for many Americans. It's not so much a concept as it is an emotion, yet people treat it as both. Is it possible to truly not be racist, to defy the structural coding that our society has abided by for centuries? Maybe. But for those lamenting over what they can possibly do, there is one comfort; the urge to reject the basis of current discrimination based on simple skin color shows that you inherently know that the idea of race is utterly ridiculous. Sure, this made up concept has real consequences, but the fact that people are fighting it shows that there may be promise yet to be found in society's development. The problem lies in eroding the power of the caste system, which goes far deeper than the concept of race. Caste is based in structure, rank, power, and wealth. Race is a concept. Caste is a system, and a deeply ingrained one. It's the basis of societal structure, and it's going to be much harder to change this system going forward.

CHAPTER 7: THROUGH THE FOG OF DELHI TO THE PARALLELS IN INDIA AND AMERICA

India was a far different world than I'd ever seen. Hazy skies, traffic going every which way with a strange logic that only the locals seemed to understand, temples and altars lining the roads as we drove. I thought of the young woman killed at the Charlottesville rally just a few months before. India and the US are two countries that are very different, yet share a similar parallel in history, coming from social hierarchies and castes separating commoners from highborn throughout the ages, using force to keep the lowest castes in servitude and driving out the natives of their lands long before. Both countries have made strides in erasing the lines between the castes throughout the last several decades, with India getting a headstart in the 40's, but the castes in both places are still evident with shadows of former codes and beliefs that are older than the current states of the countries.

Resistance to the new beliefs and codes comes heavy and change comes slowly. The upper castes in both countries are unhappy about the change and fight to keep their places of power. The castes operate differently from one another, but their structures are almost identical; keep the high caste in power and the low caste in servitude. Unlike the US, where physical differences form the basis for caste, in India, it's all about surnames. A person of low caste will typically have a Dalit surname, while the higher caste will have Brahmin surnames, the names of the gods. It also goes back to ancestors and their own statues to determine the rank of a person and knowing all this is crucial. They believe one's lot in life comes from the karma of a previous life and it's said that this belief is widely accepted by those born into their lots.

This isn't entirely true, however, and it disregards the one truth of all humans, in that freedom is desired by all. The Dalits weren't happy with their lot and neither were African Americans. So they fought the system. They felt a kinship with the lower caste of American people and welcomed them when they came to visit a few years before. They all came to know the words to the song "We Shall Overcome."

CHAPTER 8: THE NAZIS AND THE ACCELERATION OF CASTE

The Nazis took inspiration for the caste system they created by looking at the one America had founded and built on, a means to prevent Jewish influence from seeping into the Aryan nation they were trying to build. America's fascination with preserving racial purity and eugenics is ultimately what helped shape the Nazi regime as the Third Reich gained more power and control. Lothrop Stoddard and Madison Grant were well known eugenicists who despised Jews and black people. Hitler too took notice of an envied and admired America's power, taking his inspiration for his own plans for Germany. America at the time was the leading source of racist inspiration that many Americans, to this day, are unaware inspired many tragic and ghastly events during WWII. Hitler, much like a currently stationed leader, had never held office before he took control and he sought to use Democracy to destroy itself. He and his inner circle worked to turn Germany against the Jewish populace, disempowering them and demoralizing them entirely.

Everything racially legislated was based on existing American laws, such as schooling, birth and death certificates, jobs, facilities, and more. In fact, he found so much racial segregation going on here that even he felt that America had gone a bit overboard with it. They even worked tirelessly to enact a marriage ban for all Jews and Germans, preventing intermarriage. America for the most part is entirely unaware of just how much its own broken reliance on the caste system inspired much of the travesty of the Germans' treatment of the Jewish people in the forties. The one and only American legislation toward intermixed races they couldn't reconcile was the one-drop rule, wherein in America, a person considered to have even one drop of "negro" blood was considered black. Yes, that rule was considered too harsh for the Nazis.

CHAPTER 9: THE EVIL OF SILENCE

The ash from the crematoriums in the camps would often float down onto the towns outside of them, blanketing the homes and the roofs of the houses. The people did their best to ignore it, trying not to think of it for what it was. A theologist named Deitrich Bonhoeffer was recently dispatched within the walls for daring to speak out, challenging the villagers that to stay silent in the face of such evil was to embrace the evil.

In small southern towns in America, regular events called lynching's draw crowds of white people to witness justice performed against criminal black individuals. Whether they were actually guilty was never considered. Their words were never heard in their defense. Leaders bickered casually over body parts while their owner was still alive to witness. Offenses warranting death were severe; frightening white women, speaking out of turn, winking, and so on and so forth. Lynchings were seen as a pastime and no one thought anything to be wrong with it. Photos and souvenirs were taken of the bodies in sometimes horrid conditions.

If for whatever reason the crowds were denied their black victims, they'd turn hostile. They would burn buildings, sabotage firefighting equipment and then forcefully drag their victims out by force, stripping and beating them before hanging or burning them in their 'vengeance'. Again, any innocence was never considered. They were black and accused so they must have been guilty. Henry Fonda, who would go on to become a known voice of reason character in his movies, gained this inspiration from witnessing such a horrifying sight as a child.

PART THREE

THE EIGHT PILLARS OF CASTE

There are considered to be several rules or pillars set in place to keep the caste system afloat. Some of these live on today, others don't. On these following principles, a caste system is created and maintained.

Pillar 1: Divine Will and The Laws of Nature

This is the belief that all human positions in life are governed by a higher power, determined by our actions perpetrated in a previous existence. Some people are created to be of higher position than others. People have relied on this belief of a cursed sect of people to justify the kidnapping and enslavement of certain groups for centuries. Even now when slavery has been over for over a hundred and fifty years, they use it to try to maintain the caste.

Pillar 2: Heritability

The belief that a caste can be upheld based on the belief that some hereditary traits are more favorable and "better" than others, that because you were born to a certain caste, you are to remain there indefinitely, regardless of your accomplishments, simply because you look a certain way or were born to a certain people.

Pillar 3: Endogamy and the Control of Marriage and Mating

The rule that dictates that members of one caste are forbidden from marrying, having relationships with, or procreating with another member of a higher born caste. For instance, in Nazi Germany, Germans were forbidden from having any sort of intimate relationship with Jews, regardless of the reason. Lower castes are even viewed as threats to the sanctity of their "purer" bloodlines. Even a hint of a romantic interest could have dire consequences for the lower caste member involved, and higher caste members were usually never punished or reprimanded.

Pillar 4: Purity Versus Pollution

The higher caste believes itself pure and perfect and greatly fears pollution from the lower castes, in the most literal sense. During the time before the civil rights movement, when blacks and whites were kept so much apart in almost every facet of life, people believed that they could actually be polluted by a black person. Pools and lakes were kept 'separate', often by straight up imaginary boundary lines that, when crossed, resulted in severe punishment for the black offenders. People who possessed mixed blood were considered impure as well, and even those who didn't look black, but were known to have "black blood" in their veins, were considered to be black and thus, impure and lower caste. The lower caste held the responsibility of adjusting their lives to fit the standards of the higher caste, and all blame for any transgressions fell to them.

Pillar 5: Occupational Hierarchy: The Jatis and the Mudsill

A mudsill is a support beam connected to the central framework of a house. This is also the name for the bottom caste at the base of the social framework. When it came to occupations, the lowest castes were considered born to fulfill the lowliest and most repugnant of tasks, such as tanning and farming. They weren't even allowed to practice any form of art with a specific license, which cost a small fortune back in the day. The dominant caste didn't have to pay such a fee.

Pillar 6: Dehumanization and Stigma

One of the most important of the pillars for the caste system was the constant reminder that the lower castes were not to be seen as human, and children of the higher caste were taught this from a young age. If you want to pit a group against someone, just convince them that they aren't the same species as they are. They were stripped of everything they owned or were, or that individualized them. In the most extreme cases during the Holocaust, their clothes, hair, occupations, and even their names were taken from them, rendering them as little more than animals in the eyes of the Nazis. They were given only enough food to survive for the most part. African slaves were even forced to ignore natural emotions, such as sadness or grief as they were separated from children, parents and spouses at auction blocks. They were punished just for being human.

Pillar 7: Terror as Enforcement, Cruelty, as a Means of Control

Violence and terror proved the only way that many in the upper caste could control those beneath them. The threats of beatings, of injury and of death kept the terrified captives in line and within the whims of their overlings. African slaves could expect anywhere from four hundred lashes for even minor offenses. Jews in camps were whipped for killing rats to supplement their meager diets. Even after slavery was outlawed in the US, blacks were still terrified of white people, since many of the rules remained.

Pillar 8: Inherent Superiority Versus Inherent Inferiority

Even without the slavery threat hanging over their heads, many blacks today are subtly taught by society that they are 'inferior' to their white counterparts, either through dialogue or presentation in media. This is why the image of black face in old cartoons is seen as offensive and tasteless by many today, as it was once an image of ugliness and lower grade. Similarly, blacks were forbidden from using the same appliances and facilities as whites, forced to use a perceived 'inferior' object, as judged to match their given stance in life.

PART FOUR

THE TENTACLES OF CASTE

CHAPTER 10: CENTRAL MISCASTING

It was London and the weather was gray. I was attending a conference on the topic of the caste system, determined to add to my repertoire of knowledge on the subject and hopefully, provide a little of my own conjecture. I watched panel after panel, seeing more and more parallels with America as the subject of the Indian castes were brought up. Even though legal discrimination was now illegal in both countries, it's clear that a lot of work still needed to be done. I listened to stories of low caste members of Dalit (black in the US) and Adivasi (Native American in the US) being murdered by police. I wanted a copy of some of the papers of the statistics for further reading.

The professor I approached, an upper caste Indian woman and asked. She told me to wait and asked me why I wanted them. I told her my reason, but she directed me to another of her colleagues, who was too busy to speak with me. Ironically, I encountered an apparent caste system even among a group of apparent equals. I met a man who came from a second caste family in India, who once questioned the inequality and was told to keep his mouth shut and that castes were created by God. He was frustrated by the lack of answers and had given up his religion in his struggle to end caste. He also seemed puzzled about the American caste system. I told him that I was a part of the lowest caste system, and recognition shown in his eyes. He told me of his sister, who was darker than the rest of their siblings, and the struggles she went through to find marriage just because of her appearance. We had been miscast and were struggling to right the perceptions society had of us because of it.

CHAPTER 11: DOMINANT GROUP STATUS THREAT AND THE PRECARITY OF THE HIGHEST RUNG

American mortality has been decreasing in recent years, especially among middle aged white people. It wasn't illness or accidents, many of these people were taking their own lives. Advancements in longevity were rendered meaningless thanks to so many suicides. And for what purpose? All signs pointed to a decrease in life quality created by wage stagnation since the 1970's. Americans were dying of despair as they realized they could no longer support themselves and there were no safety nets to help them.

This series of insecurities was given a name: Dominant Group Status, brought about a shift in demographic superiority and the rising number of immigrants coming in for work, as well as the emergence of a black president. This inversion led to a group of people who viewed their statuses as being threatened. These people committing suicide would've been classed in the past as the higher rung in the caste system, losing their former "comfort" of being held in higher esteem than their black counterparts. It can be said that these people are dying as their illusions of grandeur died alongside them. They believed that this shift in equality made them fall closer to the bottom rung than they ever believed possible, and that the black man would dominate over the white.

It's true that this perceived inequality between former caste rungs was just too much for some people to take. A lot of programs and opportunities are now more equally available to all people more than they've ever been before and for those who grew up believing the caste system to be the golden rule, this paradigm shift is just too much to take. And even with this new mindset, many subtle programming techniques and biases held fast in the new society. People are now being biased without even realizing they're doing it. This includes medical and health related policies, housing, and insurance. The overtreatment of the caste has now become the undertreatment, a baseline of society that many of us aren't aware of, yet exists all around us. And some people are so dead set on not supporting an inversion to the caste system, subtle as it may be, that they'd rather die than support something like the Affordable Care Act. And sadly, many did.

CHAPTER 12: A SCAPEGOAT TO BEAR THE SINS OF THE WORLD

Hebrews used to sacrifice two male goats, only one of which would be killed to appease the Lord. The one that lived was lavished with the sins of the people and then cast into the wilderness, leaving the people to thrive in peace. The goat took on the blame of the collective people, as well as the blame of the misfortune they received. In a caste system, the role of the burden was given to the lowest rung instead. A functioning caste relies on a scapegoat to take all of its worries and blame away from higher members. Poor harvests, bad returns, bad weather even, all were blamed on the unfortunate lowest rung of people in the caste. After the Civil War, the newly freed slaved were blamed for the massive loss. Long after their enslavement, blacks were still seen as scapegoats almost collectively by whites. Even today, blacks in possession of marijuana are imprisoned while the substance is collected by white and converted into useful products that gain them tremendous wealth through CBD.

The scapegoat belief isn't healthy for either side, however. In 1989, when a random bullet struck a passing car, killing the pregnant woman within and resulting in the ultimate death of her premature baby, a manhunt began for the described "raspy voiced black shooter". A black man was found with a criminal record and held to the violent outcry of the people, while the husband's own suspicious behavior was ignored, such as the insurance policies he'd taken out, the unusually long time it took to drive to the hospital after the shooting while he called dispatch and how he never once comforted his dying wife during the call. He was also found to have admitted to not wanting the baby she carried. It was later found out that the man's brother, Matthew was involved in the shooting and that the man himself had shot his own wife. Matthew eventually confessed, leading to his brother committing suicide. The man had used the caste system to his advantage, knowing that if he implicated a black man, the community would riot in his defense and he'd get away scott free.

In 2016, a black man was killed by a package bomb on his doorstep in Texas. Authorities actually put forth the idea that the man had detonated the package himself and that there was nothing malicious about this apparent "prank". Ultimately, after three more bomb packages were detonated killing several more black and Latina people and injuring others, police finally took it seriously and a man was finally identified as unemployed 23 year old Mark Conditt, a conservative Christian. He blew himself up before he could be arrested. Even though the police apologized, the blacks and Latinos of the community were left angry and resentful of how much time had taken before the police took the threat seriously, and especially of how they tried to blame the first man for his own death by package bomb.

Bottom line; scapegoats are seen as expendable, their losses tolerable. To anyone with a racial bias, it's not such a terrible thing when terrible losses affect those perceived to be "lower caste". They cannot see these people as human and therefore, cannot feel the same empathy as someone who does see them as human.

CHAPTER 13: THE INSECURE ALPHA AND THE PURPOSE OF AN UNDERDOG

Dogs are pack animals and rely on the presence of an alpha in order to feel safe and secure in their worlds. Take away the alpha, and you wind up with an insecure and aggressive dog who doesn't know what to do with itself. We use similar parallels in our own behavior with terms like alpha male, underdog, etc. A true alpha is silent, using subtle, soft cues to mark their dominance in the pack. They don't need to raise their voice to command authority. An alpha is the most assured and confident, while still being reserved and quietly wielding of their power. So if you encounter a person who claims to be an alpha while yelling, screaming, and bullying others to submit to their will, you can rest assured that they're absolutely no alpha. He uses fear and aggression to maintain a position he's utterly unqualified for.

I saw this in my own dog after the divorce and he lost the alpha, my former husband. After consulting a behaviorist, I was advised to get another dog for company. After this, my dog bullied and terrorized the new dog until one day, she growled at him as he tried to shove her from her food bowl. From that day on, the tiny Havanese was in charge and the Westie followed suit as a happy beta to her alpha. These same concepts apply to humans in some regards, since we've taken so much inspiration from the way dogs run their packs, but we've also appeared to have missed a few cues, such as again, an "alpha" thinking he's top dog because he yells a lot. That's not at all how it works. People living under such an "alpha" can often sense that he's not fit for the job and will act discontented and anxious, whereas an effective and true alpha will create peace throughout those in his pack and lead them properly.

Now for the underdog and the importance of one; the omega of the pack acts as sort of a glue that holds everyone together, with frustrations being taken out on it without actual aggression starting up. The pack will actually mourn the death of an omega, laying around listless and depressed afterward. With the loss of this stabilization, the pack is severely threatened. Humans could learn a lot from wolves and dogs in assigning pack roles not based off money and birthright, but on personality traits and behavior. Many true alphas are overlooked because of color or sex while many betas are often put in leadership roles they're not suited for, also because of color or sex. The sooner we learn that personality is what matters over appearance, the better off we'll be.

CHAPTER 14: THE INTRUSION OF CASTE IN EVERYDAY LIFE

Black parents face a unique challenge with their young children; explaining the caste system to them and forcing them to face the reality that many in this country see them as a threat. How do you break a child's world like that? Do you tell them outright and make them live in fear of the first blow? Or do you just wait for something to happen on its own and shatter their world for you? What a choice. It's never too early to learn this tragedy, either. After all, Tamir Rice was only twelve when he was shot to death by police over a toy pellet gun in a legal carry state.

In the olden days, black parents had little say or custody over their own children, who were often reprimanded, taught, or even straight up taken by their white overseers. Though the beatings over parents' protection of their children have stopped, many white people still feel the subconscious conditioning to intervene on behalf of black children from their parents even today. The caste system is as strong as ever, subtle though it may be today. Children are special, however. They know instinctively that they're human and that they want to be treated as such. There are many old cases where slave children would grow aggressive to protect their parents from violence at the hands of overseers. When the civil rights era finally began, black parents finally gained a true modicum of control and protection over their children. But the caste conditioning is still there and it's constantly thriving about who is "perceived" as superior, even down to which skin color gets killed first in a horror movie.

One of the biggest offenders is the perception of roles based on skin color and this is a big one to fight. Following 2016, role policing on black people became more rampant than ever. Viral videos of white people calling the police on black people for the most mundane things. A recent one was of a black woman having the police called on her for the crime of sitting underneath a tree on church property. A black man who was babysitting two white children was followed and harassed for hours by a white woman who called the police on them. The news interviewed the older girl who said that for all the world knew, the man could've been their adoptive father. When black citizens are having their lives disrupted for their skin color alone and what some people perceive as incorrect for that skin color, then the caste system is clearly still in full throttle and function.

CHAPTER 15: THE URGENT NECESSITY OF A BOTTOM RUNG

The greatest threat to the caste system is the event in which the lower caste succeeds, which upends everything the caste system stands for. It was put in place to make sure the bottom rung never succeeds in life and stays in their designated station. In WWI, when American aid of black and white soldiers came to France, the American white soldiers were flabbergasted when the French treated them all equally instead of favoring the whites over blacks. Military command actually broke from combat to inform the French of race protocol. The French, while baffled at the absurdity in priorities, was forced to cave, noting that this "indulgence" was a grievous concern. Even when several black soldiers showed supreme bravery in the fight, dying in action, and even when several whites broke the caste to nominate them for posthumous award and decoration, they were denied this honor. Both men received lower ranking compliments and awards, one of which was lost for half a century.

During WWII, another black man was harangued and arrested for inconsequential charges, blinded by officers who beat him terribly, and then registered as guilty for disorderly conduct. He was denied medical treatment and remained blind his entire life. Whenever blacks in the lower caste sought to improve their situation or rose to success in their business ventures, history shows that many were often taken down by angry mobs. If the black owners fought back or defended themselves, they risked violence both to themselves and their employees and establishments. Many businesses and homes were destroyed for such events. Many black men were murdered for the simple fact that they were better businessmen than their white counterparts. Blacks were often denied credit for their own ideas and inventions. The idea of vaccinations came from a black man called Mathers, who was severely attacked and had his house burned at the thought of trying to inoculate people against smallpox. However, the idea thrived and by 1750, vaccinations became commonplace. But the credit was given to a white man and Mathers was more or less forgotten.

Rewards and privileges are heaped on the white man's ideas while minority ideas have to fight three times as hard to receive any sort of recognition or accreditation. Rarely did they have any room to consider themselves in a place beyond their assigned rung on the ladder, which naturally only made them keep fighting harder. Even worse, if two blacks were competing for a role in a job, the least competent one would be hired instead, preventing a more successful and talented individual from showing off what they'd learned and accomplished. The Nazis did the same with the Jews during the days of the Third Reich, keeping them from possibly overcoming the Aryans. Today, news outlets routinely pour out slews of stories in which African Americans are placed at a disproportionately high level of crime and poverty, preventing us from truly understanding their situations and how they actually compare to the strife and poverty of white people as well. Any success they receive is criminally largely ignored and this needs to change if we want to cripple the caste system.

CHAPTER 16: PACKED IN A FLOODING BASEMENT

The richest and most powerful live up high, while the lowest caste lives in the unstable below, where all the poorly maintained foundation lies. It's common knowledge among those in the higher floors to keep close watch on those in the lower floors and prevent them rising up. If any should try, the whole floor is alerted and people grow alert and paranoid. Even among the lowest caste, those with desirable features are often at risk, such as women, especially to those in power on the higher floors. This can lead even to violence and distrust among those at the bottom because they have no outlets through which to vent their frustrations. Those at the upper floors only commonly tolerate the rising to success of those from within their own ranks. They rationalize this as a scarcity of resources better left to the upper caste, when in reality, there is no scarcity at all. There's more than enough to go around, but to share would disperse the power, and so they keep it to themselves.

Snitches of planned rebellion down below is heavily rewarded by the upper caste. This has always been the case, such as with the Third Reich and slave drivers in old plantations. People left behind in the basement try to tug at the people succeeding in ascending from this station, trying to escape themselves. It's not that they resent him succeeding, they fear being left behind. This stretches even to the justice system, where one's color may very well earn them shorter and more lenient sentences. Even with advancements made to make more fair the justice system, things are still rough for those still struggling in a basement. This even applies to immigrants coming in from other countries. They don't want to be demoted like the natives of their new home, and so have to fight tooth and nail to maintain their station even when it's clear they have all the means to do so. This can even cause friction between native

African Americans and immigrants, who may feel resentment at the opportunities the latter may have had overseas. And when these lower caste people are given genuine reward and benefit for betraying their own kind, then imagine how difficult it must be for them to gain a real form of solidarity they need so badly.

CHAPTER 17: ON THE EARLY
FRONT LINES OF CASTE

A black couple who had been studying in Europe returned to America in 1933 and passed into Jim Crow Mississippi. They were aware of the social order and of the self-deprecation they'd have to go through if they wanted to survive. It was bad during this time. A lynching had just taken place over the rape of a white woman by a black man that even had many white locals in skepticism and disbelief. Allison and Elizabeth were well learned, well-educated and respectable. They were there to secretly study the caste system in its entirety, without alerting the locals to what they were doing. They were meeting two white comrades who would aid them. They were all four anthropologists there to get to the very heart of the racial division in the south. They carefully mingled, taking caution to follow the rules. The friends could never be seen together or speak together in public. Facilities were severely restricted, as were living conditions. They took pains to meet in secret to go over their work together without being caught. Their meetings were somehow found out, but not intervened with. They learned they were being watched. They protected their notes by mailing them out in safety, with Allison doing as few mailings as possible to avoid a black man arousing suspicion by posting too often.

The result of their work as of 1941 was a 538 page volume titled *Deep South: A Social Anthropological Study of Caste and Class*, detailing all the four had witnessed and documented in that town in deep Mississippi. They described how everything worked, including the economy where a black landlord couldn't enter the front door in order to collect rent from his white tenants. It took eight years of scrutiny, financial strain, depression, and even rivalry from other researchers who couldn't learn the code properly and were ostracized for showing interest in black residents. Even after its publication, it was pushed to the sidelines in favor of other publications. Publications even arose that released incorrect information about the caste to the world, such as claims that Indian caste members didn't question their lots in life, which is unequivocally false. Even from so far back, true information has always been and will always be crucial to change. Allison Davis's work, while largely forgotten, has served as a tremendous reminder of the desire for humanity and equality and just what the fabric of America truly looks like beneath.

CHAPTER 18: SATCHEL PAIGE AND THE ILLOGIC OF CASTE

LeRoy "Satchel" Paige is renowned as one of the greatest ball pitchers in history, with a pitch that was once recorded at 103 miles per hour. Jim Crow rules prevented him from ever reaching his highest potential. Oozing confidence and talent to back up this trait, he surely would've been one of the greatest players in all of history. Joe DiMaggio himself called him the best pitcher he'd ever faced. But because of the heavy segregation, Paige never got to show the world what he could do. He played in black leagues that didn't have as much funding. He trained long and hard for his abilities, naming his long-earned and mastered pitches.

At the age of forty two, he finally got a shot at the majors when the Indians were in a deep pit of struggle. Fans from all over scrambled in to see him pitch and he became the first African American to pitch the World Series, his perfect 5-0 shutout for the Indians shooting them into the World Series. His pitching shone, and though he was beyond his prime, he did well by the Indians. He was called in time after time to pitch, even in his sixties. When interviewed, he told reporters that this was what he should always have been doing. The caste system cheating Paige out of a glorious career pitching for the major leagues. Upper caste loyalists were more willing to cripple their lineups if it meant keeping a lower rung individual in his "place".

PART FIVE

THE CONSEQUENCES OF CASTE

CHAPTER 19: THE EUPHORIA OF HATE

Camera footage captures Hitler returning to Berlin. The crowds are disturbingly happy to see him, hurling confetti and trying to reach him. Nazi flags wave throughout the throngs. People of all ages are heiling their support to him. Hitler is shown briefly. He is smiling appreciatively at what he's created, a country full of support and adoration. People are laughing in glee, celebration filling the streets.

I watched this looping footage, repulsed and sickened, unable to look away. I was unable to comprehend it, the sheer force of the evil that presented itself so convincingly as a force of good. The Nazis would never have gained so much clout in the world if the Germans didn't believe in them as a force of good. They knew what carnage they supported. They knew what horrors awaited the country. It was already beginning. Some of the people who worshiped Hitler and his ideals are still living. They'll be old now, nurturing grandchildren and I find it doubtful that many of them might not still be singing his praises softly to them as they fall sleep, instilling in them the same hatred they felt so many years ago. And this is the truth of this evil; it's not just one person or even a group of people. It's the darkness in our own hearts that can be unlocked so easily and that is taught to us silently from those around us in our most formative years.

CHAPTER 20: THE INEVITABLE NARCISSISM OF CASTE

Through birth, a lower caste rung member is forced to view the upper caste as the ruling caste, whether they accept it or not. Everyone below the ruling caste is measured and assigned. In the upper caste, they're surrounded by acceptable versions of themselves in media, with few daring or caring to question how and why this is and how it affects those below them. Only some will deign to walk in the shoes of those below. Without any effort toward it, the people of the upper caste inadvertently gain a sense of narcissism and isolation from the lower caste. This superiority can be felt from all castes in one form or another.

They're even "trained" to search for closeness to the higher caste as a means of gaining height, no matter how small, such as mentioning certain physical traits one relative may have had. This sense of self importance stretches far back into history, as far back as the Greeks from which the term Narcissism originates in the form of a man who fell in love with his own reflection. The upper caste are trained to see that they are blessed with "superior" blood, even though no words may actually be spoken. Representation in media can speak volumes, for instance, about the perception of "better" in a world of racial tension. Evaluation is everything and it comes in different levels and volumes. But when people become self-inflated as a group, you run the risk of entering fascism, leading them to seek out leaders who share these same dangerous ideals. They think "I may be poor, but at least I'm white." It may be hard for some upper caste Americans to figure out where exactly they fall in line in the caste, as many of them are white and that's often all they need to know. And this is where the confusion needs to stop. And yet if they get started discussing countries of origin and the place their blood started, they might find a tiny sliver of understanding of the lower caste systems as they discover connections to old bloodlines that might just be considered "superior".

CHAPTER 21: THE GERMAN GIRL WITH THE DARK, WAVY HAIR

In WWII, Jews gradually disappeared until none remained in public. With them missing, mistrust and paranoia entered the Aryan communities. They were obsessed with purity of features and blood. A young German girl with long dark hair and almost olive colored skin raised suspicions and doubt of her worth and lineage. Now, dark hair wasn't an immediate shot to purity. Hitler had dark hair. However, his hair was straight. Hers was wavy.

Others wondered if Persian blood had stained a pure German family. The family desperately sought their origins to console themselves over their daughter's wavy, dark hair. It should've been straight and flaxen. All Aryans were under pressure to be perfect Aryan examples, or else. The girl and her family, terrified, searched their family tree. They came up with nothing, and so despite the girl's odd appearance, they proved they were Good. The girl survived, but forever haunted by her harrowing experience. She was of the upper caste and she narrowly escaped a severe punishment for falling outside the bounds of "perfection".

CHAPTER 22: THE STOCKHOLM SYNDROME AND THE SURVIVAL OF THE SUBORDINATE CASTE

It's up to those in the center caste to learn the rules set down for them by the upper caste. No one up there is going to tell it to them, of course. They learn to watch and observe, and most importantly, keep quiet. They learn their roles, play their part and accept whatever comes their way. They're forced to see the world as it is through the eyes of the upper caste, creating a form of Stockholm Syndrome in them. It's a form of bondage by those held in line by those above them. You'll often see examples these days of black people showing compassion to whites that they wouldn't often expect to see shown upon themselves in similar circumstances.

In 2014, a picture of a young boy with a pained expression hugging a police officer went viral and while the world saw a graceful act on the part of both colored people, they failed to see the truth in that this young boy was a fairly well known hostage in his own home, forced by his two adoptive white mothers to perform publicity stunts like this to gain attention while being beaten and starved behind the scenes. His suffering only ended when his mothers drove him, themselves and his siblings off a cliff, killing them all. The truth of this "touching moment" was in plain sight and everyone failed to see it. The same applies whenever we see black people immediately extending forgiveness to white attackers or oppressors. It's not so much a pure and good nature most of the time as it is social conditioning whether they know it or not.

It's said that even if you leave the caste, the caste never leaves you. This is especially true for many Indian immigrants, a scant few of which are lucky Dalits who managed to scrape together enough funds to escape. Even despite their new freedom, if they should come across higher caste Indians in this country who had the readily available funds to escape, they often cannot bring themselves to speak with them out of sheer terror of breaking the caste.

CHAPTER 23: SHOCK TROOPS ON THE BORDERS OF HIERARCHY

Historically, blacks were forbidden from eating together with whites. The white caste would always eat first. Even if the blacks in their midst were of their equals in class, they were still prohibited from mingling. Free blacks were considered an affront, almost an insult to the caste, as if they shouldn't exist. To the upper caste, they represented a threat, a question to those still enslaved, wondering why they too couldn't achieve such freedom.

Black people have constantly endured threats of law for the crime of simply existing, whether it be traveling and apparently laughing too much, taking too much time in front of white people, or just being there, taking up space. I too experienced such degrading during a flight out of Denver, where I sought help with my case due to an injured wrist. He curtly directed me off without a second look, telling me that I'd get help at the back of the plane when I got there. I was flying business class. I told him this and he stumbled, caught in his stereotyping. Obviously, I was boarding first, since that's usually how planes are boarded these days. He staggered badly, again dismissing me as one of the other attendants offered to help me.

It's not uncommon for minorities to suffer indignities on airlines like this. A well known case in 2017 was a Vietnamese American man who was beaten and dragged off a United Airlines plane because he wouldn't give up his seat due to an overbooking and random selection of customers to boot off. He was a doctor and was urgently needed at his destination. He was violently ejected by security. He said later that he was sure his ethnicity played a part in his treatment.

CHAPTER 24: CORTISOL, TELOMERES, AND THE LETHALITY OF CASTE

Black skinned people who immigrate into America often find the caste system a real chore and sometimes even a gauntlet to adjust to. They aren't used to how they're looked at, treated, or spoken to at all. They won't be expecting how they're glanced over at work, in life, and in social circles. It's a whole new and intimidating world. What's interesting to note in this country is that many native Africans don't suffer from heart disease, high blood pressure and the like. But African Americans do, and it can't just be contributed to genetics. It's their stressful environment, the treatment they endure day in and day out.

Caste friction is proving deadly, and not just to African Americans. Studies have shown that holding onto such venomous hatred and animosity for years and years on end can have drastic consequences on blood pressure and cortisol levels. By perceiving others as a threat regardless of whether they truly are or not, the body's alarms are set off and systems react accordingly as if preparing for a physical battle. Blood flow is restricted, glucose floods the muscles, etc. You can imagine that spending every day living like this is going to strain your body tremendously. We're not built to be in battle mode continuously. It is possible to override this reaction, however, by stopping and reminding yourself that this person is just another individual, and even cooperating with them if needed.

Telomeres, a vital part of the chromosomes, have also been measured. The telomeres replicate continuously throughout one's life and the more they break down, or weather, the shorter one's life is rendered. Poor equality can result in faster weathering as people stress over how to survive, how to eat, how to pay bills, etc. This means that wealthier people have telomeres that weather more slowly, as they have less to stress about. However, it's been effectively proven that black Americans have a lower life expectancy than their white counterparts, simply for how devastatingly stressful their lives are, just because they dared to step out of the hierarchies.

PART SIX

BACKLASH

CHAPTER 25: A CHANGE IN THE SCRIPT

In 2008, the caste system was shaken to its core with the election of a black man to office. He ran a flawless campaign, was well liked by the people, had a beautiful, quintessential American family. His opponent was a beloved war hero and a decorated man, with a quirky, scatterbrained woman as his running mate. Finally, the value of homes across the country plummeted, resulting massive financial loss. Obama's mantra during this rough period was Hope, and his followers believed in him enough to vote him in. However, his story wasn't pure lower caste rising. He was the son of a Kenyan immigrant and a white Kansas woman who spent his childhood in Hawaii. The dominant caste could see he wasn't "truly" lower caste and found it easier to accept him than they might've a normal lower caste black man off the street.

Obama's reign as president was even used as an example to show our supposed progress, that we had a black man in office like it truly meant something about how far we'd come. His votes weren't as good for his reelection in 2012. Even if his win was seen as a once in a lifetime event, it was still something extraordinary to comprehend for the people who couldn't fathom it. Many whites felt that visceral fear of loss of their place in the caste at the idea of a black man winning. Mitch McConnell, senate majority leader, was heard to proclaim that his singular goal was for Obama to be a one term president. This didn't succeed, but many heard his claim. Obama faced pressure after pressure and slight after slight against his character and remained cool and composed through all of it.

Right wing extremists began to rise, calling themselves the Tea Party. They vowed to "take their country back". They slandered the president and called for his eradication. Republicans changed election laws to complicate the process and by 2016, over 16 million voters were wiped from registration lists. Hate groups skyrocketed and attacks on black Americans began to increase. Even through this chaos, Obama managed to make headway on several goals, reshaping the country's healthcare and working to bridge several racial gaps before his term ultimately ended. He managed to guide the country from the deep recession it had fallen into in 2008. Despite all the good he did, the breach in script was too much for some upper caste members. People actually took their own lives over his reelection.

CHAPTER 26: TURNING POINT AND
THE RESURGENCE OF CASTE

The election of 2016 was seen as a major significance. Many waited with baited breath. I spoke with a friend of mine in the political scene. I was cautious with what I said. I knew that people weren't paying attention and that *he* could win. We knew deep down that things weren't as obvious as they appeared. As predicted, he won, and my dear friend lived just long enough to see it. People didn't believe it could happen. But it did. Caste must be fully understood to comprehend the bizarre things that it makes people do. This man promised in so few words to put whites back in charge without actually saying it. Sure, he had no political experience and a history of poor business decisions dogging him, but people didn't care. They wanted a man who spoke their language. They didn't care if they lost health insurance, stability in leadership or world respect. All they cared about was getting a white man in the white house.

Motivation to preserve racial identity is partially what drove this strange, albeit predictable turn of events. White people of the old mindset felt threatened when a black man rose from the hierarchy to take control for eight years. At this point, it was less a desire for leadership and more a desire to put black people back in their place. The election was a mirror, complete with cracks and smudges held up to the American face and it revealed all and then some. Factor in the foreign interference we've since proven existed, the marginalized voting, and the popular vote being dismissed in favor of the electoral college vote. Many question why so many others voted against their best interests without realizing that maintaining the caste *was* in their own perceived best interests. Country stability and safety come second to being at the top of the tier. The health and safety of their homes mean nothing against being better than black people.

People voting did whatever they had to do to protect the caste system, even if it meant electing the most unfit leader to ever take position in the white house. He said what they wanted to hear from their favored candidate. Even though Hillary won 3 million more votes than Trump, her count of white votes was lower. Even white women chose to vote racially rather than logically, at close to 53%. If this doesn't show just how dependent on racial superiority the parties have become, I'm not sure what would. And when morning came and Trump won the racial war, people celebrated. And others wept.

CHAPTER 27: THE SYMBOLS OF CASTE

Statues have been a classic symbol of power used by the upper caste to demonstrate their status. In current times, as statues dedicated to such old world ideas became threatened, white supremacists gathered in deadly force to defend them. It was truly bizarre how similar Nazis and Confederates were and even more so that the people involved couldn't see it. Swastikas and Confederate flags waved together as these people voiced their solidarity of superiority over their minority enemies. The city tried to cover the statue and someone always unveiled it again. It wasn't long after Heather Heyer was killed in a deadly rally and people visited the covered statue like tourists. Monuments to the Confederacy exist all over the US, despite having lost the war in 1865. Popular media like *Gone with The Wind* only added to the delusion that their mission was a grand one. The descendants of the enslaved didn't like living under reminders of the men who had enslaved their ancestors, but it seemed the country at large didn't care, valuing stone over flesh and blood. Even though they lost the war, the culture as a whole in the southern US didn't appear to reflect it very well.

Robert E. Lee's image is everywhere in the south. Schools, statues, buildings, monuments, etc. You can't escape the guy. He was born a classic example of upper caste, well-educated, West Point man, intelligent, and a slave-holder in Virginia. He once punished attempted escapees by lashing the men fifty times and the woman twenty, even ordering the constable to step in when his own overseer hesitated at such a brutal order. He then washed their backs with brine. He never faced justice for these or any other acts of violence against his slaves. Even after the war, he maintained his well-off station in life and his legacy lived on after his death as segregation took hold in the country. He's so celebrated down south, in fact that you'd be hard pressed to say he even lost.

Even as contractors were hired to take down the statues, white supremacists all over attacked these people personally, desperate to protect the statues. By the time the one company willing to do it, karmically a predominately black owned company, they managed to take apart an obelisk despite public trouble and sabotage from supremacists. Removal went smoother from then on and this time, cheering crowds gathered to watch a statue of Lee fall to the ground. It's a stark contrast to places like Germany, which chose to shun supremacists and bury their history as deep as they could. They even paved over Hitler's grave site. Displaying the swastika is now a crime there, and hardly anyone will admit to being related to Nazis without an ounce of shame in their voices. Even the most zealous members of the country won't glorify the horrors that Hitler committed.

CHAPTER 28: DEMOCRACY ON THE BALLOT

In 2014-2015, things were getting more tumultuous. Videos of police brutality on unarmed citizens were on the rise across the country, protests were being held everywhere, the saying Black Lives Matter made its full debut. Obama did his best to remain composed through it all, delivering a eulogy at the funeral of a pastor killed in a Charleston church massacre. His voice led through the somber Amazing Grace sung in the spirit of hope for forgiveness by a slave ship captain.

It looked as though the country was coming together. Of course, three years later, it looked to be getting worse again and I wasn't optimistic for the future. I prayed that I'd be wrong. Unarmed shootings, brutality, suppression, it all had the earmarks of a dangerous and unsettling trend. Offenders caught on tape for many of these incidents hadn't faced justice at all yet. I discussed it with a friend of mine. It was clear that Trump had brought to the surface attitudes and beliefs that had long been held by the people of this country, that black people had a place that they dare never cross. It left us questioning how many, if given the choice, would choose democracy over being white.

CHAPTER 29: THE PRICE WE PAY
FOR A CASTE SYSTEM

America may be a wealthy country, but it's far less benevolent than some of its contemporaries around the world. This is the price we pay for a caste. A system that looks after everyone is viewed here as one that takes prosperity away from individuals. Europe and Australia, both wealthy countries, seem to display a far greater sense of responsibility and care toward their fellow countrymen. In America, it really seems as though it's every dog for itself. In other societies, families don't have to sell precious keepsakes just to afford healthcare. Families don't go broke with ailing relatives in other parts of the world. So why is it so bad here?

This is the caste system, designed to build rivalry between countrymen and breed distrust, where everyone is encouraged only to look out for themselves, where kinship is a myth. America is home to more gun death than almost any other country in the world. It also has the highest incarceration rate and the mortality rate for pregnant women is ridiculous for a wealthy nation. Education is far further down than it should be and it ranks only eighteenth in happiness around the world. How the mighty truly have fallen.

To top it all off, America is now seeing the highest number of coronavirus deaths, which exposed just how broken the hierarchy of America truly is as it saw upwards of over a hundred thousand deaths in just under half a year. The mudsill jobs all remained, such as delivery drivers, baggers, store clerks, etc. All others were told to shelter in place while the government bickered over how many peanuts to throw its citizens in unemployment and stimulus checks. America's self-centered behavior had caught up to it and the country was falling apart at the seams as poor leadership on top of the already broken caste system began to take its toll.

PART SEVEN

AWAKENING

CHAPTER 30: SHEDDING THE SACRED THREAD

A man in India, born to the highest caste in the land, bore witness to his father attempt to attack a Dalit worker for not showing respect, only to retreat when the Dalit merely attempted to defend himself with a tree branch. His father cast himself from the village in shame for not maintaining his and the Dalit's station.

The boy grew up, had a family, and forgot about his father's humiliation from a system he may not have been ready for. But he was a changed person following that day. He'd always been taught that the Dalit were lazy and docile, accepting of their low lots in life. Clearly, they weren't. He came to admire and become acquainted with a few Dalits who managed to cross his path in their slightly improved stations. He admired their intellect and how capable they were, and how they actually were able to teach him things he'd never known. These people weren't pollutants, they were thinking, clever human beings like himself. He felt deep shame for the lie he and his family had lived by for generations. He shed his sacred thread, which he'd worn since his steps into manhood. Born a third time, this time into awakening, he swore to find his true self without by renouncing his caste. He began his true journey.

CHAPTER 31: THE HEART IS THE LAST FRONTIER

I hired a plumber to come and help me fix my sump pump when my basement started flooding. As I half expected, but hoped not to see, he was distant and unhelpful with me. Now, obviously I'm used to this, but it still hurts having to endure it at unexpected times of every day. Rather than get angry, I tried a softer approach.

I mentioned how I'd lost my mother the week before. I asked him about his. His had been gone for a long time. I recounted how sick my mother had been her last few years and asked him about his. We recounted some brief stories of our mothers and I watched as he turned noticeably friendlier. He got my sump pump cleaned out within minutes. In this short time we'd bridged a societal gap using a common thread; the first loves of our lives. He eventually found that my water heater had gone bad. He shut off the water to the heater and charged me sixty nine dollars for the visit. Minutes after he'd left, he came right back and asked if he could shut off the gas to the heater as well to save to me some money until I could replace it. He happily did his work, knowing his way around, chatty and friendly. In that moment, he was family. He told me with relief in his voice how much worse it could've been. Then, he happily bounded out of the old house.

EPILOGUE: A WORLD WITHOUT CASTE

Our world is tiny, insignificant and invisible in the grand tapestry of the universe. Our time on this world is brief, so brief that it's honestly tragic. We yearn to be something bigger, something better than what we've known. The false divisions of caste have harmed our species tremendously. The Nazis and the terror they brought with them, the Civil War and its single minded desire to enslave a sect of people, all those who died whose gifts have been forever lost because of their tragic end. Just think of where we'd possibly be if we valued the gifts and brilliance of all people equally.

When Albert Einstein and his wife were driven from Germany to America, he was horrified to discover yet another caste system waiting for him. Having discovered the awful practices as a mature man who had grown up knowing they were wrong, he was sickened by what he saw happening to blacks of the era. While he lived in the states, he visited an opera house where Marian Anderson, an extremely talented lower caste born singer was performing to an enormous crowd. But for all her acknowledged talent and skill, she was forbidden to rent a room in the town, to which Einstein and his wife Elsa offered her to stay in their home. Even when the inns reversed their policies on black Americans, she continued to stay with her beloved friends. Einstein always refused to accept the American way of life of looking down on those deemed inferior. Being a Jew himself, he found it difficult to impose his own treatment onto others. He regularly spoke out against this treatment, teaching black children his theories of relativity, and more. He hated prejudice because he'd experienced it firsthand.

The things a caste judges us for are things we have no power to change or control. Who we are inside doesn't account for what we happen to look like. Regardless of where we're born in the caste, we don't have to let it shape us. We can choose our own paths within it. This book isn't trying to resolve every problem the caste has stuck us with, but to shine a light on it and expose it for what it is; a broken, unfair system that only hinders us. As we speak, in just a few decades, whites will be outnumbered by minority people in America. Even though this would have little material effect, many white people are reacting in fear to this occurrence already. We need to reach some sort of enlightenment about our precarious situation now before things get even worse for both sides. It can and has been done. Germany did it, and their problem was astronomically bad during WWII. We've even done it ourselves to a small degree by giving women more liberties and abilities they didn't have at the start of the 20th century.

There's no one simple solution. It will take a massive effort of everyone involved to make the change we desperately need. We must take a long hard look at ourselves and think about what we want to be in the future. We also need to recognize that antiquated ideas like the caste system must be let go of entirely if we want a future at all where peace is even an option. As we are now, it's not. But with change and perseverance, it could be, one day. On the day when we can look at people of all demographics and appreciate each of them for their unique talents and gifts, then we can truly say how far we've come and feel proud of ourselves as a species. A world without caste would truly set everyone free.

IMPORTANT FACTS RECAP

Prologue: The Man in The Crowd

1. A famous photograph from the Third Reich shows a single man refusing to perform the infamous Nazi salute
2. This man is believed to be named August Landmesser
3. August had been in love with a Jewish woman. The new laws forbidding their relationship soured his views of the Nazi party.
4. What does it take to be as brave in refusal as August was?

Chapter 1: The Afterlife of Pathogens

1. 2016 was a year of unrest, politically and socially
2. A strange and unusual president spent four years pulling back legislation from decades before
3. A string of violence and hate erupted across the country as a result of his rhetoric
4. Societal contagions may not be fully destroyable

Chapter 2: An Old House and An Infrared Light

1. The caste system is built on deemed 'inferior' traits to beat down and demoralize those possessing such traits.
2. With a system this old and this ingrained, getting rid of it is no short order.
3. It takes care and time to build lasting connections with others even through this old and broken system.

Chapter 3: An American Untouchable

1. Martin Luther King Jr. first saw the correlations between the caste systems of America and India while on a trip there and being referred to as an Untouchable
2. The American caste system dates back to the days of early slavery in the south with captured African slaves.

Chapter 4: A Long-Running Play and the Emergence of Caste in America

1. The caste system helped to develop the country that is America
2. America was founded on the backs of unwilling slaves
3. Slavery may be over, but the caste system has gone nowhere.

Chapter 5: The Container We Have Built For You

1. A woman met named Miss Hale was named such because black people were denied formal titles.
2. Society in the south and north has classically held different regulations and expectations for the caste system
3. While we fight for a non-racist society, the root of the problem is still very much evident.

Chapter 6: The Measure of Humanity

1. Race and caste are two different, yet related things.
2. Science has shown that we're all biologically connected to Africa and that race is a flawed concept.
3. Caste makes up the majority of structure in America and won't be eroded nearly as easily as race

Chapter 7: Through the Fog of Delhi to the Parallels in India and America

1. America's caste is very similar to India's.
2. India focused on surname caste, while America focused on skin color and race
3. The Dalit lower caste related heavily to the African Americans of America

Chapter 8: The Nazis and the Acceleration of Caste

1. Much of the rules of the Third Reich were inspired by America's own caste system
2. Hitler was known to have admired and envied America's views on other races.

Chapter 9: The Evil of Silence

1. To refuse to speak is as much considered evil as the act of evil itself.

The Eight Pillars of Caste

1. A series of rules established over the centuries about how the caste system is maintained
2. Each one is designed to dehumanize and demoralize those at the very bottom of the rung.

Chapter 10: Central Miscasting

1. The world over, skin color has become, in many places, the de facto means of judging another human being

2. People often tend to engage in caste behavior whether they know it or not.

Chapter 11: Dominant Group Status Threat and the Precarity of the Highest Rung

1. Many white Americans have begun subconsciously reacting to the caste change by succumbing to despair and ending their lives
2. The caste system has begun to change beneath the surface, with the inequity gaining new and strange progress in more extensive areas
3. Many white Americans don't even realize they're being biased

Chapter 12: A Scapegoat to Bear the Sins of the World

1. Blacks and minorities have classically been seen as societal scapegoats
2. A scapegoat is seen as expendable
3. Authorities have often been shown reacting more slowly to tragedy in the lower castes

Chapter 13: The Insecure Alpha and The Purpose of an Underdog

1. 1. Alphas of a pack are, contrary to popular belief, not loud and aggressive, but quiet and silently commanding.
2. An omega serves an important role of pack function by easing tension and stress
3. If people can learn to prioritize personality over appearance and gender, we'll be much better off with better leaders.

Chapter 14: The Intrusion of Caste in Everyday Life

1. Black people are often forced to endure intrusions into their lives based on what color they are
2. Many police calls have been made over black people doing mundane things in the last few years

Chapter 15: The Urgent Necessity of a Bottom Rung

1. Black people are often pushed out of roles that could better their stations in life
2. Historically, many black business owners were killed simply because they were successful.

Chapter 16: Packed in a Flooding Basement

1. It's part of the subliminal "programming" of the higher caste to keep the lower caste in their perceived places.
2. The caste system rewards snitches to the lower caste, those who betray their own to lift their status

Chapter 17: On the Early Front Lines of Caste

1. Early 1900's America was rife with unfair caste rules
2. An eight year study was done on the deep south, showing in great detail just what sort of oppression black people lived under

Chapter 18: Satchel Paige and the Illogic of Caste

1. Paige was regarded as one of the best pitchers ever known.
2. The caste system denied Paige a chance to pitch until he was so badly needed that they had no choice

Chapter 19: The Euphoria of Hate

1. Hitler rose to power amidst a country full of rowdy support and cheers
2. Many Germans knew exactly what Hitler was doing and they still supported him
3. Hate isn't relegated to a single person or demographic, but to what we are taught to unlock in our deepest of hearts.

Chapter 20: The Inevitable Narcissism of Caste

1. The upper caste system is faced with a phenomenon of narcissism in their "superiority"
2. White Americans might find it harder to locate their place in the caste
3. White people must rely on their blood connections to figure out country of origin

Chapter 21: The German Girl with the Dark, Wavy Hair

1. Even those in the upper caste are bound by rules of perceived perfection
2. Anyone found wanting of these rules faced potential severe punishment

Chapter 22: The Stockholm Syndrome and the Survival of the Subordinate Caste

1. On a more subliminal level, lower caste members are conditioned to behave a certain way whether they know it or not
2. Forgiveness creates absolution for the upper caste and is often expected

3. The caste never fully leaves the subconscious once its burrowed in

Chapter 23: Shock Troops on the Borders of Hierarchy

1. Blacks and other ethnicities often receive poor treatment while traveling
2. Very little can be done to correct this behavior

Chapter 24: Cortisol, Telomeres, and the Lethality of Caste

1. Studies have shown that the constant stress endured by black Americans is shortening their lifespans
2. Studies have also shown that harboring hate and animosity for other ethnic groups can have lasting damaging effects on our bodies.
3. It's possible to override these automatic responses by reminding ourselves that these people are all just human

Chapter 25: A Change in the Script

1. The first black president was as historical as it was controversial.
2. Obama faced opposition from many threatened white groups over his skin color alone
3. Despite strong opposition, Obama still managed to pull the country out of the recession and reshape healthcare practices
4. Election laws were changed following his inauguration

Chapter 26: Turning Point and the Resurgence of Caste

1. The election of 2016 was a major significant event for what it represented

2. The electoral college won out over the popular vote, in which Hillary won.
3. People actively voted against their best interests, choosing instead to vote for a racial interest

Chapter 27: The Symbols of Caste

1. Symbols of caste are commonplace in areas where it's heavily supported
2. Taking down even one statue of Robert E. Lee proved extremely dangerous
3. America and Germany share similar pasts, yet Germany has openly worked to accept responsibility and shun anyone who still carries the delusions of the Third Reich

Chapter 28: Democracy on The Ballot

1. The 2010's were a period of tumultuous violence and protesting
2. The racist attitude was only getting worse, hinting at a repeat of history

Chapter 29: The Price We Pay for a Caste System

1. America ranks extremely low in happiness, health, and public security.
2. The pandemic rendered America unprepared to handle it and exposed how broken the country is
3. The caste system, designed to create rivals and competition, has stripped the country of what it needed to weather the pandemic strongly.

Chapter 30: Shedding the Sacred Thread

1. The caste system is little more than human invention and can be ignored
2. No one in the caste system is any more or less human.

Chapter 31: The Heart is The Last Frontier

1. Common ground can be found through the simplest of memories
2. The best way to reach someone's heart is to speak of its fondest treasures

Epilogue: A World Without Caste

1. It's possible to obliterate a caste system.
2. We need to start appreciating not what we look like, but who we all are
3. A world without a caste would set everyone free

PERSONAL ANALYSIS

Going into this book, I've spent the last four and a half, five years watching the situation in America and seeing it get worse and worse. There's no denying that racial tensions spiked when Obama took office in 2008 and you don't need to be political to have noticed that, or noticed how much worse it got when Donald Trump took office in 2016. Things seriously got bad. Mass shootings throughout most of 2017, police brutality ramping up to the point where innocent people and families were being attacked, cuffed and beaten, white supremacy attacks on peaceful protests, Nazi and Confederate flags making appearances everywhere, it was a mess and still is to this day. So to read this book and get hit right in the chest about how terrible the situation is right now, I was struck with an exhausted sense of hopelessness at the fact that nothing I do as a single person can change our world.

But therein lies the answer to my worries; I'm only a single person. Of course I alone can't change anything, despite a childhood filled with heroic TV shows where single people change things every day. Growing up watching stuff like that instills a sense of empowerment in a person, it seems. Even as an adult and realizing that reality isn't so kind, I still felt that empowerment to an extent. And I realized that I'm not alone in this endeavor. Despite the news and social media wanting to convince us otherwise, not everyone is in it for their own destruction just to put the lower caste back in their perceived place. There are millions of people just like me who desire change and want to leave this world someday knowing we helped make it a slightly better place.

ACTION PLAN

So now that you have this book and the lessons it has to teach us, here's what we need to do. Fortunately for us, the answer is relatively simple; just remember that we're all people. Every one of us is a human being just trying to survive. Black, white, brown, yellow, polka-dotted, we're all running the same race together. Sure, some are in it purely for themselves and don't care who they hurt to get it, but the majority of people just want to live their lives in peace and enjoy their friends and families. Some people are irrationally scared of things that are literally not true or aren't going to happen. What we as people need to do is to not only treat all humans with the same respect we want for ourselves, but to also show kindness to those who are afraid. Perhaps all they need is a little reminder that their fears aren't bigger than they are.

The caste system can be broken. Germany successfully did it following the horrors of WWII. Any mention of activity in the devastating and evil Nazism out there is a felony and is treated as such. Our voices together are powerful and spending each day trying to do a little good in the world, it'll add up in no time. Buy groceries for your disabled neighbor, visit lonely people in nursing homes, sit and talk with someone on the bus, give to a homeless person, whatever you can think of. Remind these people that they're still human and that they matter. It may take a while, there's no denying that. But we are powerful and we are capable of change together.

DISCUSSION QUESTIONS

1. Have you ever been a victim of racism? If so, what happened?

2. Have you ever witnessed racism? What happened, and could you do anything?

3. Did you grow up experiencing the caste system as a lesson in some form?

4. America was founded on the caste system. What do you think can be done to move away from this foundation?

5. How do you feel about the violence happening around you?

6. If given the chance to stop violence happening close to you, what would you do?

7. Were you aware there was a caste system in America before now?

8. Do you think that we could be doing more to fix what's going on?

9. How do you feel racism or classism has affected your life?

10. If you could change one thing about this country, what would it be?

ABOUT HIGH SPEED READS

Here at High Speed Reads our goal is to save you time by providing the best summaries possible. We stand out from our competitors by not only including all of the pertinent facts from the subject book but also a personal analysis of the book with action plan included, easy to follow summaries of each chapter including a list of chapter highlights and even discussion questions to get you thinking.

As you can see, we go above and beyond to make your purchase a pleasant one. If you learned something beneficial from this book please leave a positive review so others can benefit as well. Lastly if you haven't yet make sure you purchase the subject book, Caste, by visiting https://amzn.to/3iLH1Gc .

Made in the USA
Middletown, DE
02 October 2020